MUSEUM OF MARVELS
ANIMAL
ACTIVITY BOOK

POLLY CHEESEMAN & VLAD STANKOVIC

ARCTURUS

ARCTURUS

This edition published in 2024 by Arcturus Publishing Limited
26/27 Bickels Yard, 151–153 Bermondsey Street,
London SE1 3HA

Author: Polly Cheeseman
Illustrator: Vlad Stankovic
Editor: Violet Peto
Designer: Jeni Child
Managing Editor: Joe Harris
Design Manager: Rosie Bellwood-Moyler

ISBN: 978-1-3988-4332-5
CH011562 NT
Supplier 29, Date 0524, PI 00006536

Printed in China

WELCOME TO THE MUSEUM!

You are about to enter an extraordinary interactive museum of animals. As you wonder through its galleries, take the time to admire the curious creatures on display, and read fascinating facts about them. Then solve the brain-bending puzzles and try doing some hands-on activities.
Most of all, enjoy your time in the Museum of Marvels ...

MAP OF THE MUSEUM

ROOM 2

MUSEUM OF MARVELS

ROOM 1

ENTRANCE

EXIT

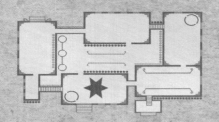

ALL ABOUT ANIMALS

From teeny-tiny insects to enormous blue whales, the animal kingdom is incredibly vast and varied. In the first part of the museum, you'll find out about different groups of animals and the things they have in common.

Match each of the animal groups to its correct description. Write the correct letter next to each animal group.

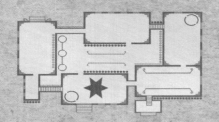

⬡ 1. INVERTEBRATES

⬡ 2. FISH

⬡ 3. AMPHIBIANS

⬡ 4. REPTILES

⬡ 5. BIRDS

⬡ 6. MAMMALS

A. These animals have feathers and lay eggs. Most are able to fly.

B. Nearly all of these creatures have hair or fur. Their babies drink milk.

C. Most of the creatures can live in and out of water. They have moist skin.

D. This is the largest animal group by far. Their bodies do not have a bony skeleton.

E. The skin of these creatures is dry and scaly. Their babies hatch from eggs.

F. These animals live underwater. Their bodies are covered with scales.

Can you figure out which group of animals each of the creatures below belongs to?

Fill in the letter code for each animal.

I = invertebrate
F = fish
A = amphibian
R = reptile
B = bird
M = mammal

How many of each group can you spot?

Invertebrates: _____

Fish: _____

Amphibians: _____

Reptiles: _____

Birds: _____

Mammals: _____

7

INCREDIBLE CREEPY-CRAWLIES

Invertebrates are creatures with no backbone or skeleton inside their bodies. Arthropods, such as insects and crustaceans, are invertebrates with an "exoskeleton." This is a tough outer layer that protects the animal's soft body parts inside.

Instead of an exoskeleton, some soft-bodied invertebrates have a shell to protect themselves.

Invertebrates such as beetles and worms help to break down plants and add nutrients to soil.

Can you spot seven differences between these two invertebrate displays?

8

Can you complete the picture of this monarch butterfly?

There are well over a million different types of insect—more than any other animal group. Most insects have six legs, two pairs of wings, and a body divided into three parts.

Insects such as bees and butterflies feed on nectar from flowers. As they fly from plant to plant, they spread pollen, which helps new plants grow.

Rearrange the letters to spell out four pollinating insects.

THOM

FRYHOVEL

MEBLUEBEB

EBELET

UNDERWATER CREATURES

Amazingly, invertebrates make up around 97% of all animals on Earth. Many invertebrates live in the oceans, rivers, and lakes. They range in size from single-celled creatures to the enormous giant squid.

Can you complete the jigsaw puzzle? Which piece doesn't fit?

Some crustaceans, such as shore crabs, live in and out of water. Others, such as shrimp, spend their lives beneath the surface.

Anemones and jellyfish belong to a group of invertebrates called "cnidarians." They use stinging tentacles to catch tiny prey, as well as to defend themselves.

Shellfish such as mussels and scallops open their shells under the water. They feed on algae, which they filter from the water.

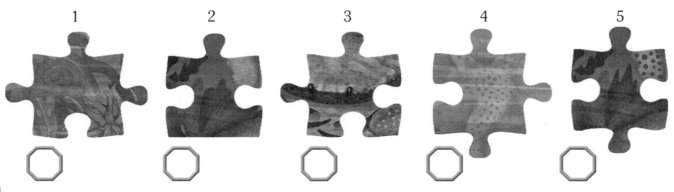

1   2   3   4   5

Complete this picture sudoku by placing one of each sea creature into every row, column, and minigrid.

Invertebrates are the most ancient creatures on Earth. Sea sponges, for example, have existed for around 600 million years—that's long before dinosaurs lived.

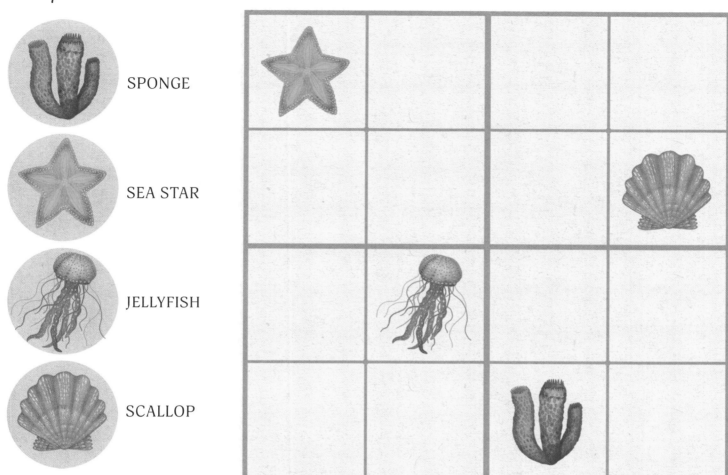

SPONGE

SEA STAR

JELLYFISH

SCALLOP

Can you figure out which of the silhouettes matches the main picture of the squid?

A

B

C

D

At up to 13 m (43 ft) long, the giant squid is the world's largest invertebrate. Squid have eight arms and two longer tentacles, which they use to catch prey.

FABULOUS FISH

There are thousands of different types of fish living in the world's oceans, rivers, and lakes. Fish have skeletons inside their bodies, and most have scaly skin. Fish breathe using their gills, which take oxygen from the water.

Fish use their dorsal fins to stay upright. Other fins help fish change direction or stop. Moving their tail from side to side pushes them through the water.

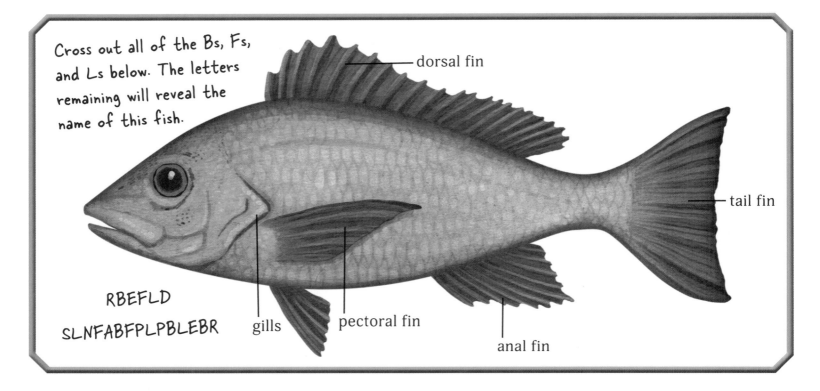

Cross out all of the Bs, Fs, and Ls below. The letters remaining will reveal the name of this fish.

dorsal fin

tail fin

RBEFLD
SLNFABFPLPBLEBR

gills

pectoral fin

anal fin

Some fish swim together in a large group called a school. This makes it harder for predators to pick out individual fish.

How many Atlantic herring can you count in this school?

Most fish are cold-blooded, and their bodies are the same temperature as the water. Some fish live in warm waters, while others are adapted to live in the cold, deep ocean. Fish come in many different shapes and sizes.

Read the fact files, then put the fish in size order from 1 to 5, with 1 being the largest.

OCEAN SUNFISH

EATS: Jellyfish
HABITAT: Mild and tropical oceans
SIZE: Up to 3.3 m (11 ft) long
DID YOU KNOW? Ocean sunfish use their fins to "row" through the water.

OARFISH

EATS: Plankton and small sea creatures
HABITAT: Cool and deep ocean
SIZE: Up to 11 m (36 ft) long
DID YOU KNOW? Due to their long bodies, oarfish have been mistaken for sea monsters.

GREAT WHITE SHARK

EATS: Seals, dolphins, and other sharks
HABITAT: Coastal ocean waters
SIZE: Up to 6 m (21 ft) long
DID YOU KNOW? A great white shark can swallow a seal whole.

WHALE SHARK

EATS: Plankton
HABITAT: Warm ocean waters
SIZE: Up to 20 m (46 ft) long
DID YOU KNOW? Despite having thousands of tiny teeth, whale sharks cannot bite or chew.

HUMPHEAD WRASSE

EATS: Fish, coral, and sea urchins
HABITAT: Coral reefs
SIZE: Up to 2 m (7 ft) long
DID YOU KNOW? Humphead wrasse can live for over 30 years.

1 ....
2 ....
3 ....
4 ....
5 ....

AMPHIBIANS

Frogs, toads, and salamanders belong to a group of animals called amphibians. Most of these cold-blooded creatures can live in and out of water. Their skin is moist and thin, which allows amphibians to take in oxygen from the water.

Frogs and toads may look similar, but they have differences. Frogs spend more time in water than toads, and they have wetter, smoother skin, and longer legs.

Match these frogs into pairs. Can you spot the toad hiding among them?

Most amphibians lay their eggs in water. Young amphibians have gills to breathe underwater and look very different to adults. As they get older, many amphibians develop lungs that allow them to breathe air.

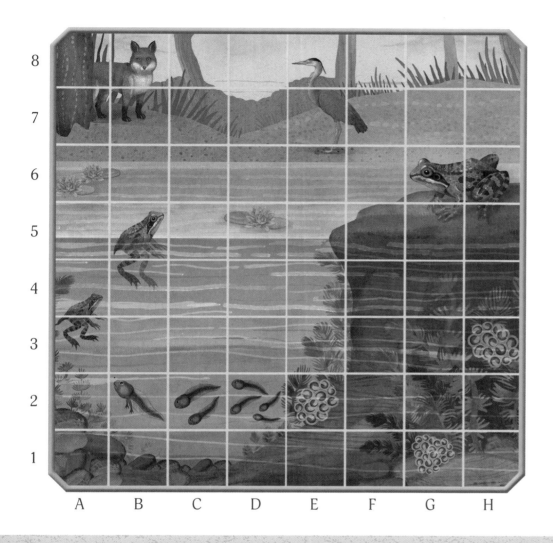

Can you find the items below in the picture? Write the coordinates of the square or squares they are in.

FROG SPAWN

TADPOLES

WATER LILY

Some unusual-looking amphibians can be mistaken for other creatures, such as reptiles or fish.

Can you guess which of these creatures is NOT an amphibian?

NEWT

MUDSKIPPER

CAECILIAN

AXOLOTL

REMARKABLE REPTILES

Lizards, snakes, and turtles are all reptiles. These animals are known for their dry, scaly skin. Reptiles are cold-blooded, so they rely on their surroundings to control their body temperature. Basking in the sun keeps reptiles warm and healthy.

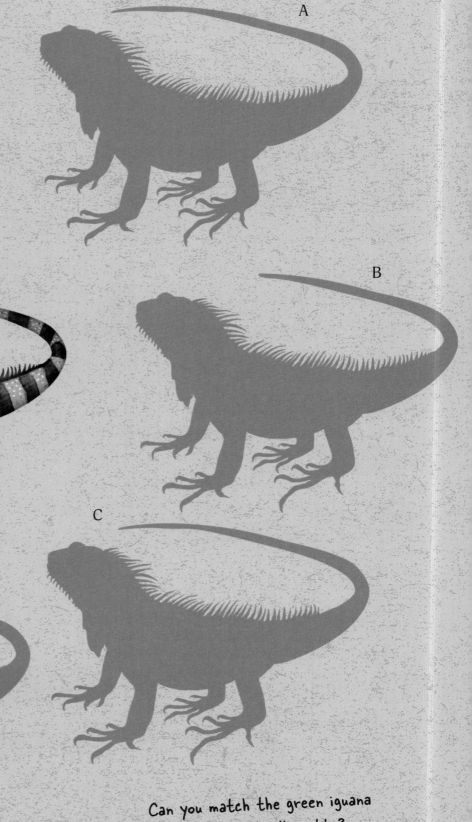

Can you match the green iguana to its exact silhouette?

Reptiles need to shed their skin. This makes space for the reptile to grow and gets rid of old scales. Snakes wriggle out of their old skin, leaving it in one long piece.

Draw some more scales to complete the snake picture, then finish with your brightest pens and pencils.

The scales on a snake overlap each other, allowing the skin to be smooth and flexible.

Guess which picture comes next in each of these reptile and egg sequences.

Nearly all reptiles hatch from eggs. Most reptile mothers leave their eggs to hatch and fend for themselves. When baby reptiles hatch, they look like tiny adults.

BRILLIANT BIRDS

Birds live all over the world—from the freezing Polar regions to the grasslands of Africa. All birds have wings, feathers, and bills, but they come in many different shapes and sizes.

Count the flamingos in this colony. Can you spot the flamingo facing a different way to the others?

Flamingos live in large colonies near shallow water. They are known for their bright pink feathers and huge, curved bills. Like other wading birds, flamingos have very long legs.

A

B

C

D

E

F

G

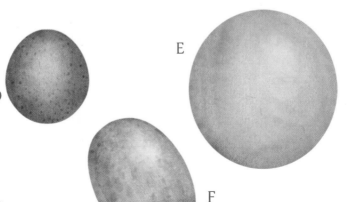

Put these eggs in size order from 1 to 7, with 1 being the largest.

All birds hatch from eggs. Most birds will build a nest to lay their eggs in. Usually, parents sit on the eggs to keep them warm until they are ready to hatch.

Ostriches lay the largest eggs in the world. They can weigh the same as 27 chicken eggs!

Birds are the only animals to have feathers. Soft, fluffy feathers keep birds warm, short body feathers keep them dry, and long flight feathers help them fly.

This bird is an expert at flying, reaching a top speed of 111 kph (69 mph).

Cross out all the letters that appear twice. The remaining letters will spell out the bird's name.

A P P S B W C E I A F X B C T X E

Can you complete this sudoku? Each flightless bird must only appear once in each row, column, and mini square.

Although all birds have wings, not all birds can fly. Penguins are perfectly adapted for swimming and diving underwater. Other flightless birds, such as ostriches, can run extremely fast.

KĀKĀPŌ

PENGUIN

KIWI

OSTRICH

A WORLD OF MAMMALS

The type of hair a mammal has is suited to the place it lives. Can you match these mammals to their correct descriptions below?

Mammals are warm-blooded animals, and their babies drink their mother's milk. Most mammals have hair or fur on their bodies, which helps keep them warm. Whether it's on land or in water, mammals are found all over the world.

A. PANDA

B. MOLE

C. HIPPOPOTAMUS

D. ARCTIC HARE

E. ZEBRA

F. SEA OTTER

1. This huge mammal likes to wallow in lakes and rivers in Africa. It has hardly any hair.

2. In summer, this animal has brown fur. It grows a thick white coat in winter, keeping it warm and safe in the snow.

3. This burrowing mammal has short, velvety fur. Its hairs can lie at any angle, letting the animal go back and forth underground.

4. This mammal spends most of its life in the water. It has thick waterproof fur and long whiskers.

5. This mammal's thick, dense fur keeps it warm in its cold forest home in the mountains of China.

6. This animal lives in African grasslands. Its striped coat makes it hard for predators to pick it out from the rest of the herd.

All mammals breathe air. Even mammals that spend their lives in water, such as dolphins and whales, must come to the surface to breathe.

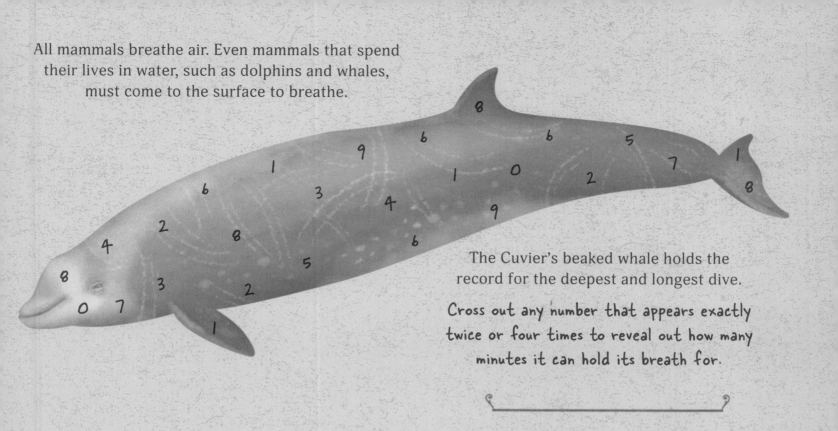

The Cuvier's beaked whale holds the record for the deepest and longest dive.

Cross out any number that appears exactly twice or four times to reveal out how many minutes it can hold its breath for.

FLYING FOX

Can you guess which of these mammals is a type of bat?

Although some mammals jump or glide from tree to tree, bats are the only mammal, that can truly fly.

FLYING SQUIRREL

FLYING LEMUR

HABITAT EXHIBITION:

RAIN FOREST

Tropical rain forests are hot and wet throughout the year. These lush habitats are home to an amazing variety of animals. Beautiful birds fly through the canopy, while other creatures swing, slither, and scuttle over the dense vegetation.

The biggest rain forest
in the world is the
Amazon Rain Forest in
South America.

Search the rain forest scene,
and see how many of these
creatures you can spot.

BULLET ANTS are insects that can
give a very painful sting.

RED-EYED TREE FROGS have
sticky pads on their feet that help
them climb wet and slippery plants.

SPIDER MONKEYS get their name
from their long, strong tails and limbs.

MACAWS are
noisy parrots.
These bright
birds feed on
fruit, nuts,
and seeds.

TREE RUNNER LIZARDS scuttle up
tree trunks, hunting invertebrates.

What other animals can you find?

23

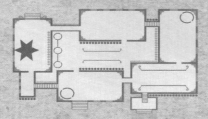

What type of food do these animals prefer? Write the correct letter next to each animal.

WHAT ANIMALS EAT

Plants make their own food by taking energy from the Sun.
To get their energy, animals must find or hunt food.
Herbivores are creatures that eat mostly plants, carnivores eat
other animals, and omnivores eat both plants and animals.

C = carnivore   O = omnivore   H = herbivore

1.

2.

3.

4.

5.

6.

7.

8.

9.

24

Z	N	O	M	L	A	S	B
T	A	G	B	I	T	B	E
Q	I	R	A	C	Z	S	R
Z	Q	U	E	E	T	Y	R
T	D	S	R	O	K	G	I
O	N	U	O	F	F	S	E
I	G	R	A	S	S	E	S
E	S	O	O	M	R	V	M

Grizzly bears are omnivores that feast
on a variety of different foods.
Can you find some of their foods
in the wordsearch?

MOOSE   BERRIES
INSECTS   GRASSES
SALMON   ROOTS
FRUIT

Some animals feed on creatures that have already died. Others eat dead and rotting plants or even animal poop!

Cross out the letters S, C, and A to find the names of these two scavenging creatures.

SCASVSASUCSCLSASTCUSCRSASE

SDACSCUSANCG CBSESECTASLASEC

25

FOOD CHAINS

Animals can be linked together by the foods they eat, in what is called a food chain. The chain usually starts with a plant, which is eaten by an animal, which is eaten by another animal, and so on.

Can you match the animals below to the gaps in the food chains?

MOUSE

SEA OTTER

LION

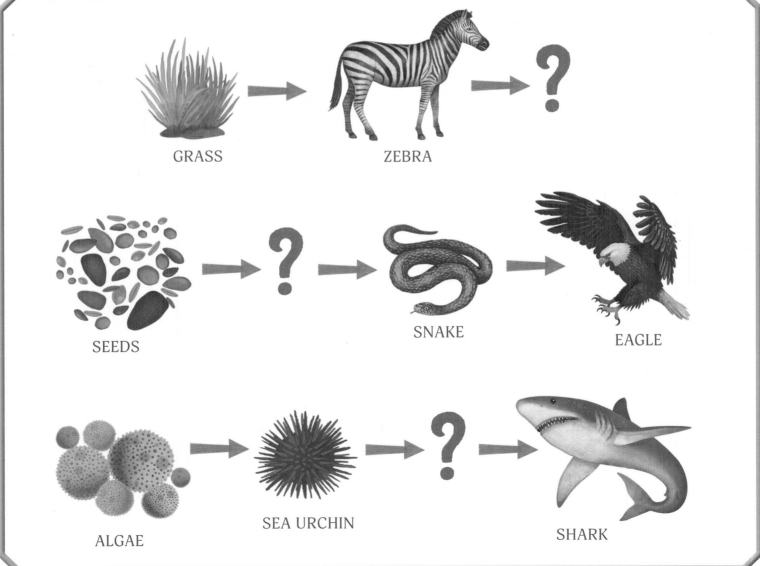

GRASS → ZEBRA → ?

SEEDS → ? → SNAKE → EAGLE

ALGAE → SEA URCHIN → ? → SHARK

The animal at the top of a food chain is usually a carnivore. An animal that isn't hunted by anything else is called an apex predator.

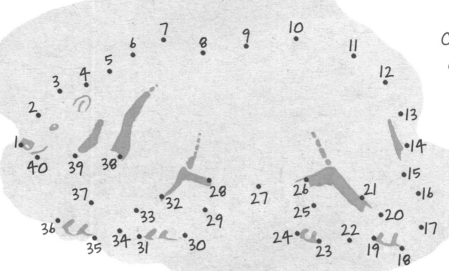

Connect the dots to discover what this apex predator is.

Many animals eat more than one type of food, so they link into lots of different food chains. These interconnecting food chains are called food webs.

FOX

KESTREL

STARLING

RABBIT

SHREW

GRASSHOPPER

GRASS

CATERPILLAR

Look at this food web, then see if you can answer the questions below. Hint: The arrows mean "is eaten by."

1. Which plant is shown in this food web?

2. Which animals have no predators?

3. Which foods does the shrew eat?

PREDATORS

Meat-eating animals have many cunning ways to get their next meal. Some predators rely on speed to chase down prey, others prefer to use surprise tactics.

Although roadrunners can fly, these super-speedy birds prefer to hunt on foot. They sprint after prey such as small mammals, lizards, and even venomous snakes!

Solve the problem below to find out how many steps roadrunners can take in just one second:

$$17 - 7 + 4 - 2 = \underline{\qquad}$$

Praying mantises wait perfectly still until an insect comes close, then they grab it with lightning speed. Their front legs have gripping hooks and spines, so prey cannot escape.

Can you spot the praying mantis that perfectly matches this one?

B

A

C

Ambush hunters lie in wait, watching their prey closely for the best time to strike.
When they see a chance, they leap out and attack.

Tigers have striped coats that allow them to hide in long grass and stalk their prey. Powerful jaws and sharp teeth deliver a deadly bite.

This tiger wants to sneak up on its deer prey. Can you work out the best place for it to hide by following the instructions?

Start at 1A.
Go up 1 square.
Go right 2 squares.
Go up 1 square.
Go right 2 squares.
Write the coordinates here: ⌊_____⌋

Komodo dragons are the world's largest lizards. As well as feeding on dead animals, they attack prey such as goats, deer, and even other Komodo dragons. Their powerful legs make them surprisingly fast.

Which of these Komodo dragon statements are true, and which are false?

A. Their mouths are full of serrated teeth that grip and tear flesh.
B. Their saliva is packed with toxic bacteria, which can kill prey within 24 hours.
C. Their jaws contain a venom that stops blood from clotting, causing massive blood loss to prey.

TEETH AND CLAWS

You can tell a lot about what animals eat by looking at their teeth, claws, or beaks. An animal's teeth are suited to the foods they eat. Flat teeth are good for grinding up plants, and pointed teeth are perfect for stabbing and ripping meat.

Sharks are known for their many rows of terrifying teeth. When a shark loses a tooth, a new one moves forward from the row behind to fill the gap.

Great white sharks have around 50 teeth in their mouths, some measuring 6.5 cm (2.5 in) long.

How many shark teeth can you count here?

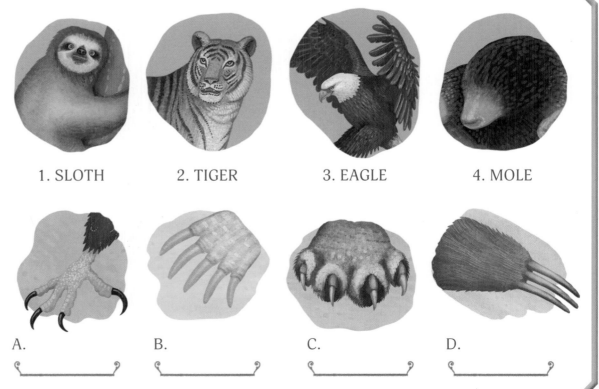

Some animals have long claws for climbing trees or for digging underground. Predators, such as big cats and birds of prey, have sharp claws that are used for gripping and ripping meat.

Can you match these creatures to their claws?

1. SLOTH   2. TIGER   3. EAGLE   4. MOLE

A.   B.   C.   D.

Crocodiles have enormous jaws filled with between 60 and 70 cone-shaped teeth. Crocodiles cannot chew their food. Instead, they snap their powerful jaws to crush the bones of their prey.

Look at the top picture, then copy the contents of each square to draw your own crocodile in the grid below.

FINCH

TOUCAN

OSPREY

FRUIT

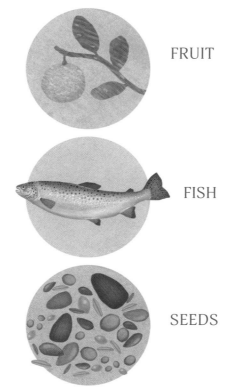

FISH

SEEDS

Instead of teeth, birds have bills, or beaks, that come in all shapes and sizes. Short, powerful beaks are suited to cracking open seeds. Long bills can reach fruit high up in trees. Sharp, hooked beaks are perfect for tearing flesh.

Can you guess what these birds eat by looking at their beaks? Draw lines to match each bird to its dinner.

HERBIVORES

Animals that mainly eat plants are called herbivores. Some herbivores munch on a wide range of plants and plant parts, including leaves, roots, seeds, and fruits. Other creatures prefer to eat just one plant, such as grass.

Pandas only eat bamboo, a type of tall, treelike grass.

Look at the clocks below to figure out how many hours a day this panda spends eating.

08:00 AM to 12:00 PM

Hours:

01:00 PM to 04:00 PM

Hours:

05:30 PM to 10:30 PM

Hours:

Total hours =

Mountain goats are expert climbers. They feed on mountain plants such as grass, moss, herbs, and ferns.

If each of these adult goats has two kids, how many goats in total are there in the herd?

Buffaloes are grazers, which means that they are animals that mostly eat grass. They live in large herds, which helps protect them from predators.

BUFFALO

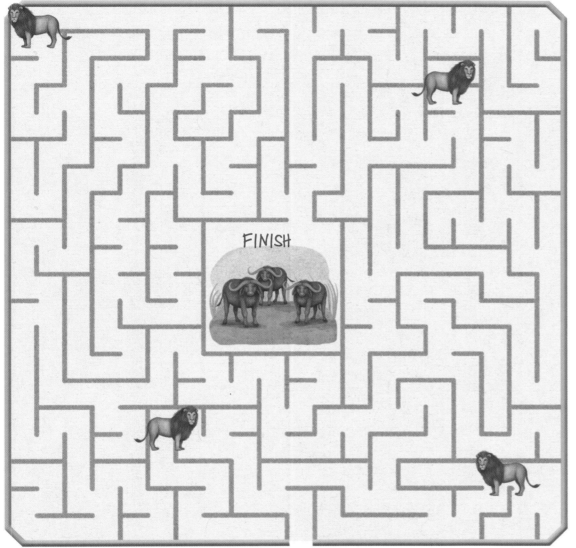

FINISH

START

Help the buffalo get through the maze to the safety of the herd. Be sure to avoid the lions along the way!

LION

Animals that eat fruit include orangutans, fruit bats, and many types of birds. Can you guess what an animal that eats mostly fruit is called?

A. Fruitigan   B. Fruitivan   C. Frugivore

HUNTING IN GROUPS

Can you put the picture segments in the correct order to create the orca hunting scene?

Most predators like to go it alone, but some animals work together to make a kill. It's thought that animals can catch more prey if they hunt in groups than they would do hunting alone. A hunting group may also be able to tackle larger or trickier prey animals.

1. 2. 3. 4. 5.

② ◯ ◯ ◯ ◯

Orcas, or killer whales, are clever mammals that live in groups called pods. Orca pods hunt by herding prey into small areas before they attack. They also swim together to create large waves that flip seals from sea ice into the water.

Spotted hyenas live in large groups called clans. Spotted hyenas are skilled hunters. They hunt in groups of up to 25 when targeting large animals such as zebras. Hyenas use their senses of sight, hearing, and smell to find their prey.

Spotted hyenas have powerful bone-crushing jaws. They can eat up to a third of their body weight in one sitting!

Clan 1

Clan 2

Clan 3

Read the clues, and check the boxes to find out which hyena clan caught which type of prey.

Clan 2 did not catch small prey.

Clan 3 did not catch a striped animal.

Clan 1 caught an animal with horns.

	ZEBRA	WILDEBEEST	HARE
Clan 1			
Clan 2			
Clan 3			

Pack hunters, such as wild dogs and wolves, signal to each other and try to surround their prey. When working as a team, wolves and dogs can take down animals much larger than themselves.

NAME: AFRICAN WILD DOG
LIVES IN: Africa
PACK SIZE: up to 60
HUNTS: hares, warthogs, antelopes, and wildebeest

NAME: GREY WOLF, OR GRAY WOLF
LIVES IN: North America, Asia, and Europe
PACK SIZE: up to 36
HUNTS: squirrels, moose, and reindeer

NAME: DINGO
LIVES IN: Australia
PACK SIZE: up to 12
HUNTS: rabbits, wallabies, and kangaroos

Read about these different canine hunters, then match each one to its silhouette.

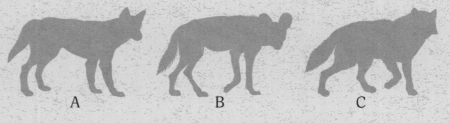

A   B   C

PROTECT AND DEFEND

The natural world is a perilous place, and animals are always on the lookout for danger. From bony plates to supersharp spines, some cunning creatures have clever ways to protect themselves from attack.

Can you decide which of these statements about amazing armadillos are true and which are false?

Armadillos are covered with bony plates that act like a protective shield. When they are attacked, armadillos roll into a ball or pull in their feet. Their outer "shell" keeps their soft body parts safely tucked away from would-be attackers.

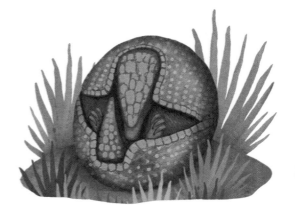

1. Armadillos are strictly vegetarian.
   True   False
2. Although they look like reptiles, armadillos are actually mammals.
   True   False
3. Armadillos live in very cold climates.
   True   False
4. Armadillos use their long, strong claws for digging underground.
   True   False

Turtles and tortoises are reptiles that have hard shells for protection. The shells are made of keratin—the same substance as our fingernails. Tortoises live on land, but many turtles spend their time in water.

Study the two pictures. Can you work out which is a sea turtle and which is a land tortoise? Hint: Look at their feet!

A

B

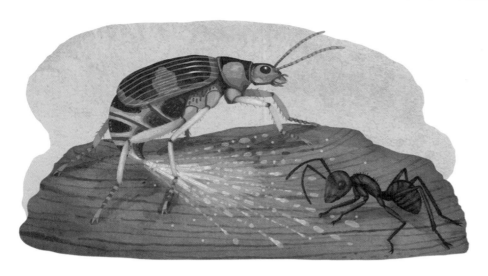

Some creatures defend themselves by launching an attack! When threatened, bombardier beetles fire a boiling, poisonous liquid out of their abdomens. The liquid weapon is strong enough to blind, or even kill, an attacker.

Can you spot 7 differences between the two pictures of a bombardier beetle defending itself from a hungry ant?

Surgeonfish look harmless, but they have a small razor-sharp spine on either side of their bodies. If a predator swims too close, they can inflict a nasty wound with just a flick of the tail.

A	B	C	D	E	F	G	H	I	J	K	L	M	N	O	P	Q	R	S	T	U	V	W	X	Y	Z
	4	5						11				16												27	

Complete the key, then use the code to discover the name of the surgeonfish's sharp spine.

21	5	3	14	18	7	14

HABITAT EXHIBITION:

POLAR

Despite the freezing temperatures, many animals survive in the chilly Arctic. The icy waters are home to many different fish and sea creatures. Mammals have a thick layer of fat under their skin, which helps keep out the cold.

Polar regions have just two seasons—summer and winter—but both are extremely cold.

How many of these animals can you spot in the icy Arctic scene? Draw some extra polar creatures on the ice!

WALRUSES are a type of seal. Their huge tusks put off potential predators.

HARP SEALS live in large groups. They hunt fish and other sea creatures.

POLAR BEARS are always on the lookout for seals to eat. They are the largest land carnivores.

ORCAS, or killer whales, are a type of dolphin. They prey on seals and young walruses.

ARCTIC COD produce a special protein that keeps their blood from freezing in the chilly Arctic Sea.

39

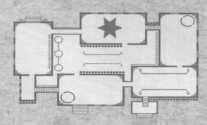

A SENSORY WORLD

All animals experience the world through their senses. For people, that means through sight, hearing, smell, taste, and touch. Other animals' senses can be very different. Senses enable creatures to find food and avoid danger, and they are adapted to the environment the animals live in.

Can you match these creatures to the descriptions below?

Some creatures have razor-sharp vision, while others can detect sounds or smells from far away. Can you match these creatures to the senses they are known for?

◯ 1. SNAKE   ◯ 2. BAT

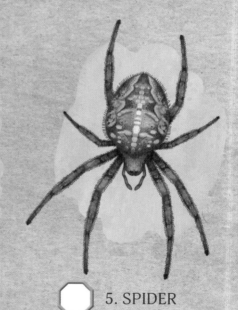

◯ 3. POLAR BEAR   ◯ 4. OWL   ◯ 5. SPIDER

A. Large eyes give this predator razor-sharp vision when hunting small mammals at night.

B. This creature can feel the tiniest vibrations in each of its many legs.

C. Large ears enable this nocturnal mammal to hear the movements of tiny insect prey.

D. This creature flicks its long, forked tongue to "taste" chemicals in the air around itself.

E. This meat-eating mammal can sniff out a seal's breathing hole in the ice from 1 km (half a mile) away.

Animals' senses are used together to gain as much information as possible about their surroundings. Foxes use their excellent senses of hearing, sight, and smell to find prey and escape danger.

START

FINISH

Follow this sequence of fox eyes, ears, and noses to help the fox find its way back to its den.

PUZZLE TEXT:
You can only move up, down, left, and right.

1   2   3

Some animals do not use all of the five main senses. Creatures that live in caves, deep underwater, or underground may not need to see particularly well, so their other senses become more important.

Which trail leads from the naked mole rat to its plant root dinner?

A
B
C

Naked mole rats spend their lives in underground burrows. They are almost blind and deaf, so they use their senses of smell and touch to get around.

ANIMAL VISION

Most of the information we receive about our surroundings is through our two eyes. In the animal world, things can be very different. Spiders usually have eight eyes, starfish have five, and some creatures have many more.

Scallops are sea creatures with a hard shell. They have lots of tiny blue eyes, just inside their shells. Solve the equation to reveal how many eyes scallops can have.

59 x 2 + 82 = _____

The pupil is the dark part in the middle of the eye that lets light inside. Animals' pupils can be vertical or horizontal, round, or even W-shaped.

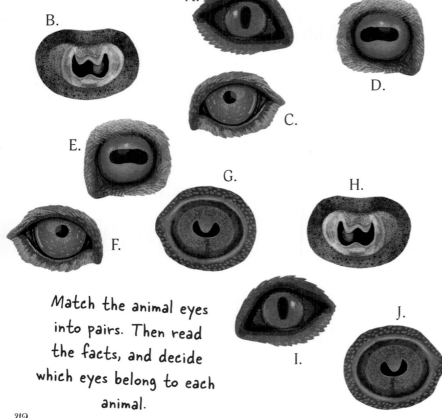

A.

B.

C.

D.

E.

F.

G.

H.

I.

J.

Match the animal eyes into pairs. Then read the facts, and decide which eyes belong to each animal.

1. Vertical pupils help smaller predators, such as FOXES, judge distance. The pupils widen to let in more light when hunting at night.

2. Round pupils provide good all-around vision during the day. They are common in the eyes of larger hunters, such as LIONS.

3. Horizontal pupils give grazing animals such as GOATS a wide view of the land around them, even with their heads down in the grass.

4. CUTTLEFISH have distinctive W-shaped pupils that help them balance light and dark particularly well.

5. Crescent-shaped pupils, like those of CATFISH, help creatures see clearly underwater.

Use your brightest pens to complete the beautiful dragonfly picture.

Some dragonflies have up to 30,000 lenses in each of their compound eyes.

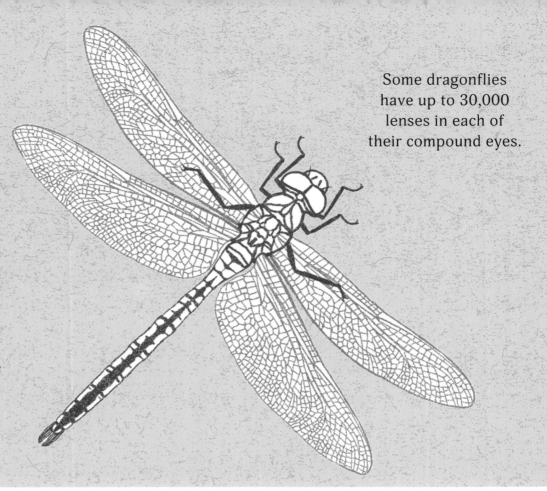

Insects have compound eyes with many thousands of tiny lenses. Compound eyes enable insects to notice quick movements. The eyes cover most of the head, so insects can see all around themselves.

Male bowerbirds build elaborate twig structures to attract a mate. They pile up small objects close to the structure and place larger ones in front. This tricks the female into thinking that the bower is bigger than it is.

A.

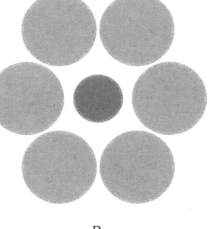

B.

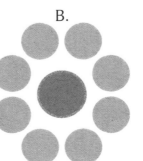

Information coming in through the eyes is processed in the brain. Sometimes our eyes convince our brains that something is different to how it really is. These are optical illusions.

Look at the two images on the left. Which blue circle is larger, A or B?

HEARING AND SOUND

Sounds are made when objects vibrate, sending invisible waves through the air. The waves are picked up by our ears and changed into messages that go to our brain. Some animals have very sensitive hearing that is adapted to their food and environment.

Some bats have a growth on their snout that helps to direct sound. Cross out the letters B and T to discover the name of this fleshy growth.

BNTOTBSBE - TTLEBABF

_ _ _ _ - _ _ _ _

Bats use their excellent sense of hearing to listen out for prey. Some bats have enormous ears that collect more sound waves. Bats also use sound to find their way around in the dark. This is called echolocation.

Find out more about echolocation on pages 52–53.

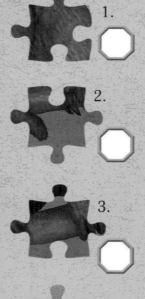

1. ⬡
2. ⬡
3. ⬡
4. ⬡

Howler monkeys use sound to communicate, making one of the loudest calls of all animals on Earth. Their whoops warn other howlers to stay away and can be heard up to 5 km (3 miles) away.

Can you complete the jigsaw puzzle? Which piece doesn't fit?

Match each animal to its fact about hearing.

Although many creatures can hear, they don't all have fleshy outer ears like humans do. For example, birds have excellent hearing, but no visible ears. Mammal ears work in a similar way to ours, although they can look very different.

1. It has the largest ears of all animals compared to its size. Its ears are so sensitive that they can hear insects burrowing under the desert sand.

CARACAL

AFRICAN ELEPHANT

2. This animal communicates with sounds such as barking and howling. Its ears can move independently of each other to hear noises up to 16 km (10 miles) away.

LONG-EARED JERBOA

3. This animal can make and hear very low sounds. It uses its enormous ears to hear across distances of 10 km (6 miles).

HARE

4. A relation of the rabbit, this fast creature uses its very long ears to listen out for predators, such as foxes.

WOLF

5. This type of wildcat has tufted ears that can swivel around to pick up sounds of hiding prey.

SNIFFING AROUND

All these animals have a great sense of smell. Read the facts, then rearrange the letters to spell out their names.

Animals use their sense of smell to find food, mates, and sniff out danger. Creatures may leave their scent behind to mark out their territory, to communicate with others, or even to defend themselves.

1. This blood-sucking insect is attracted to body smells, particularly to the stench of sweaty feet!

QUOSITOM

_ _ _ _ _ _ _ _

2. This mammal eats poisonous eucalyptus leaves, sniffing out leaves with the most nutrients and the fewest toxins.

AKALO

_ _ _ _ _

3. This meat-eating fish can smell a drop of blood from up to 400 m (a quarter of a mile) away.

KHARS

_ _ _ _ _

4. The male of this insect can smell a chemical made by a female 11 km (7 miles) away.

ILKS HOMT

_ _ _ _ _ _ _ _

5. This bird eats the bodies of dead animals. Some species can smell dinner from over a mile away.

TRUELUV

_ _ _ _ _ _ _

6. This long fish relies on its tube-shaped nostrils to sniff out prey.

ELE

_ _ _

When skunks are threatened, they protect themselves by squirting a disgusting-smelling liquid from under their tails. The stench is so strong, it can be smelled 1 km (half a mile) away.

Can you find your way through the maze, avoiding all the skunks?

START

FINISH

Elephants have the sharpest sense of smell in the animal kingdom. They are particularly good at finding water by smell. They can detect water sources up to 19 km (12 miles) away.

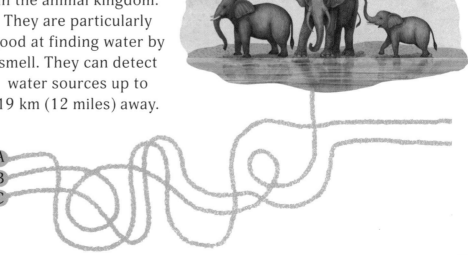

A
B
C

Which route should the elephant take to reach the watering hole?

DIFFERENT TASTES

All vertebrates (animals with a skeleton inside their bodies) have tongues with taste buds. A sense of taste tells animals if foods are ripe, fresh, and good to eat. Taste can also let animals know if food is rotten or harmful.

A human has around 10,000 taste buds, but other animals have more or fewer than this. Solve the equations below to figure out how many taste buds each of these animals has.

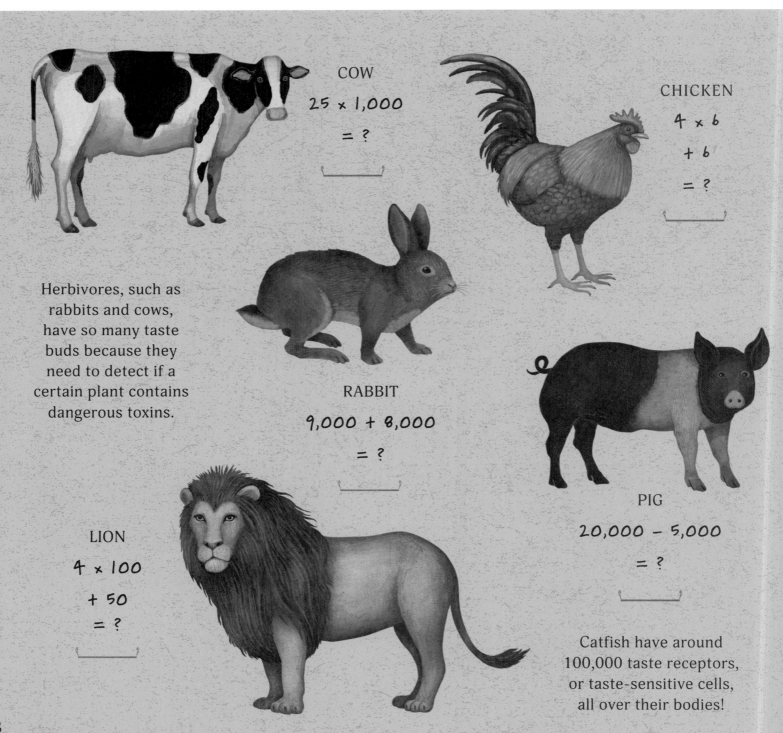

COW

$25 \times 1{,}000$

$= ?$

CHICKEN

4×6

$+ 6$

$= ?$

Herbivores, such as rabbits and cows, have so many taste buds because they need to detect if a certain plant contains dangerous toxins.

RABBIT

$9{,}000 + 8{,}000$

$= ?$

PIG

$20{,}000 - 5{,}000$

$= ?$

LION

4×100

$+ 50$

$= ?$

Catfish have around 100,000 taste receptors, or taste-sensitive cells, all over their bodies!

Not all creatures have tongues, but that doesn't mean they can't taste. Butterflies have taste receptors on their feet, which enables them to taste plants as soon as they land on them.

How many butterflies can you count on this plant?

Which half completes the picture of the octopus? Hint: Octopuses have eight arms.

Octopuses hunt by sticking their arms into gaps and holes to find hiding prey. They have taste receptors on the suckers of their arms, so they can decide if something is good to eat just by touching it.

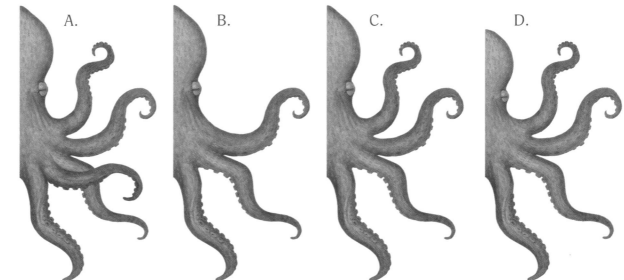

A.

B.

C.

D.

TOUCHY-FEELY

As with the other senses, a sense of touch helps animals to get around, find food, and avoid danger. Nearly all animals have touch receptors in their skin. Many creatures have touch receptors in other places on their bodies, too.

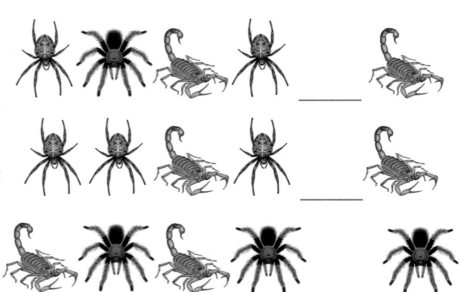

Spiders and scorpions are very successful hunters. This is partly because their legs are covered with highly sensitive hairs. These hairs detect tiny movements in the air, which helps them "feel" the presence of prey.

Can you fill in the gaps in these spider and scorpion sequences?

Cover the second picture, then study the first one for one minute.

Now cover the first picture.

Can you spot the two creatures that are missing from the second picture?

Insects and some other arthropods have a pair of sense organs called antennae on their heads. Different creatures' antennae function in different ways. Some sense touch and movement, and others use them to smell, taste, and communicate.

The sense of touch is especially important for animals that don't see well, such as nocturnal creatures and those that spend time under ground or under water.

All these animals rely on their sensitive snouts to find their way and find their food. Can you match each animal to its correct snout fact?

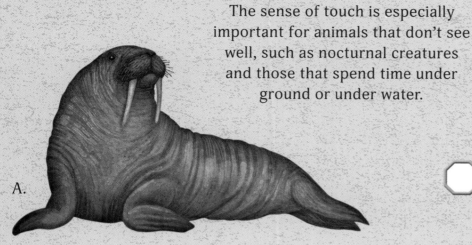

A.

NAME: Walrus
LIVES: The Arctic seas of Europe, Asia, and North America
FEEDS ON: Shellfish, such as clams

1. SENSORY SNOUT: This nocturnal animal twitches its whiskers at up to 25 times a second to map out its environment.

B.

NAME: Star-nosed mole
LIVES: Underground in wet soil of North America
FEEDS ON: Insects and worms

2. SENSORY SNOUT: Its whiskers detect faint movements in the water, which helps it follow prey.

C.

NAME: Rat
LIVES: Countryside and towns worldwide
FEEDS ON: Plants, insects, and small animals

3. SENSORY SNOUT: It uses its long, bristly whiskers to find food on the ocean floor. The whiskers can grow up to 30 cm (1 foot) long.

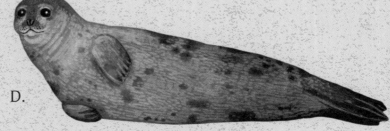

4. SENSORY SNOUT: With 22 fleshy "tentacles," this animal's nose is six times more sensitive than the human hand.

D.

NAME: Common, or harbor seal
LIVES: Northern coasts of North America, Europe, and Asia
FEEDS ON: Fish and squid

SUPER SENSES

Animals use their senses of sight, hearing, smell, taste, and touch to gather information about the environment. Some creatures have additional super senses that can detect things that humans can't.

Some animals, such as bats, whales, and dolphins, use echolocation. When they make noises, the sound waves bounce back from objects to the animal that made them. This 'echo' is used to locate prey and helps them find their way around.

Follow the instructions to help this dolphin find where it needs to be.

Start at A1
Go right three squares
Swim up two squares
Go left one square
Swim up one square
Go right two squares
Dive down one square

Write the grid reference here: _____

All creatures give off small electrical signals as they move around. Sharks, rays, and some other fish can detect this electricity with special sensors. Sharks have around a thousand electricity-sensing holes on their bodies, helping them find prey.

Can you locate the electricity-sensing fish hidden in the wordsearch?

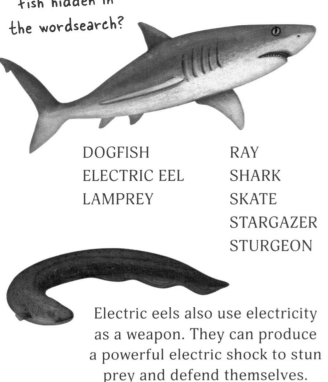

DOGFISH
ELECTRIC EEL
LAMPREY

RAY
SHARK
SKATE
STARGAZER
STURGEON

X	W	A	L	V	A	X	K	S	R	S
F	R	Z	H	A	G	A	H	T	S	T
S	A	O	S	R	M	A	B	S	G	U
D	Y	P	I	H	R	P	I	U	Y	R
H	Z	Q	F	K	E	U	R	K	M	G
Y	V	G	G	H	O	J	Y	E	H	E
S	F	F	O	W	O	C	O	U	Y	O
T	N	M	D	E	T	A	K	S	K	N
E	L	E	C	T	R	I	C	E	E	L
S	T	A	R	G	A	Z	E	R	M	D
A	D	L	F	S	Q	S	U	Z	D	Y

Electric eels also use electricity as a weapon. They can produce a powerful electric shock to stun prey and defend themselves.

Pit vipers pick up infrared radiation like a thermal imaging camera. Fill in the shapes according to the key to reveal this pit viper's next meal.

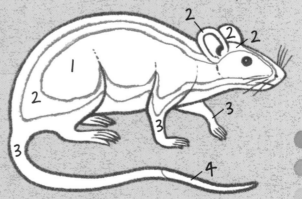

1 = red
2 = orange
3 = yellow
4 = green

Animals that hunt at night rely on their other senses to find prey. Pit vipers have a very useful extra sense that helps them see in the dark. The snakes have a pit under each eye, which detects the warmth of other animals.

HABITAT EXHIBITION:

CORAL REEF

A coral reef is a beautiful underwater habitat teeming with life. Countless creatures visit the warm, shallow waters to feed and breed. Coral reefs provide shelter and places to hide for both predators and prey.

Each coral is a colony of tiny creatures called polyps. The polyps make hard, bony layers around themselves for protection. Over thousands of years, these layers form coral reefs.

The world's coral reefs are in danger. Pollution and warming sea temperatures damage coral reefs and the creatures that live there.

Spot these creatures in the coral reef. How many of each can you find?

MANTA RAYS visit reefs to be "cleaned" by small fish called wrasse.

CLOWNFISH are immune to the stings of anemones, so the fish use them to hide in.

FINGER CORAL forms treelike branches. There are hundreds of different types of coral.

BANDED SEA KRAITS are venomous snakes. They must come to the surface to breathe.

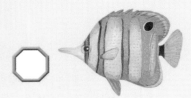

BUTTERFLY FISH have thin bodies that allow them to swim through narrow gaps in the coral.

How many sea stars are there?

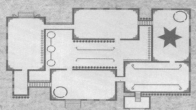
THE LIVES OF ANIMALS

All creatures go through different stages of life. They are born, they grow up, they have babies, and eventually they die. The different stages an animal goes through as it develops is called a life cycle.

Some animals, such as most amphibians and insects, completely change their form as they develop into an adult. This extreme change in body shape is called metamorphosis.

Like frogs, dragonflies begin their lives in water. Can you match each picture to its description to complete the dragonfly life cycle?

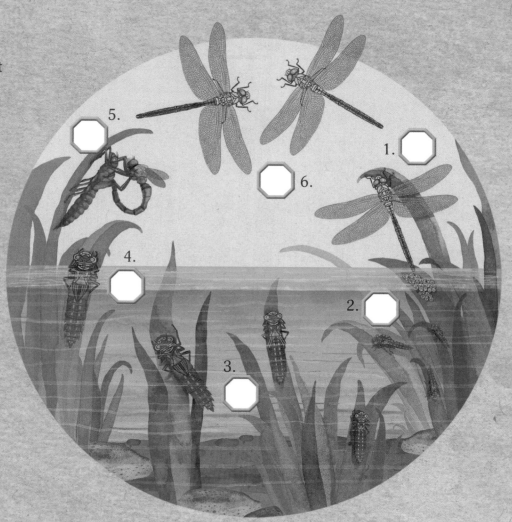

A. The adult dragonflies can now fly off to make babies of their own.

B. When they are fully grown, the nymphs climb out of the water.

C. A female dragonfly lays her eggs in the water. About a week later, the eggs hatch.

D. The adult dragonflies push themselves out of their nymph skins.

E. As they grow, the nymphs shed their skins many times.

F. Baby dragonflies are called nymphs. They live underwater, eating all they can.

While some creatures look very different from their parents, other animals are born looking like tiny adults.

Match each adult to its baby.

Now rearrange the letters in the list on the right to spell out the names for the baby animals.

ZEBRA _____ LOAF

TURTLE _____ CLANTHIGH

SWAN _____ GETNYC

FROG _____ PELTADO

BUTTERFLY _____ ALPERTCLAIR

RHINOCEROS _____ FLAC

SEAL _____ UPP

KANGAROO _____ YOJE

Mayflies spend most of their lives as underwater nymphs. After about a year, they change into an adult mayfly and live for just one day.

Humans can live to be 100 years old or slightly more, but some animals can live much longer than that.

Adwaita was a male Aldabra giant tortoise from India, but what age did he live to? Cross out all the numbers that appear twice, then arrange the leftover numbers from smallest to largest to find out.

1 2 9 4 3 4 5 7 3 1 6 9 7

ANIMAL HOMES

All creatures need somewhere to rest, shelter, hide from predators, or bring up their babies. From holes in the ground to treetop nests, animals make their homes in all kinds of curious places.

Help the hermit crab find a new home, by putting these shells in size order. Number them from 1 to 5, with 1 being the largest.

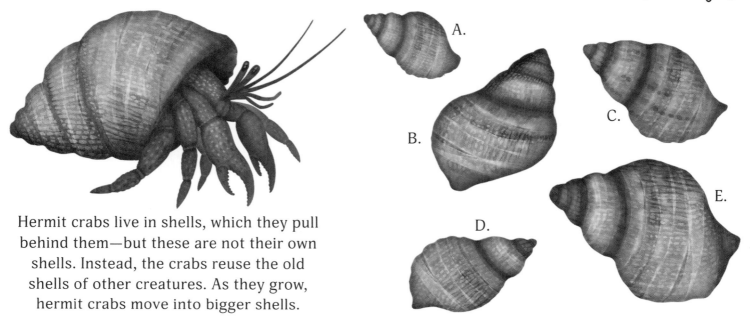

Hermit crabs live in shells, which they pull behind them—but these are not their own shells. Instead, the crabs reuse the old shells of other creatures. As they grow, hermit crabs move into bigger shells.

A.

B.

C.

D.

E.

Living underground is a way for animals to keep cool in hot climates, or warm and dry in cold weather. Burrows also keep large predators out and provide easy access to foods such as invertebrates and plant roots.

Prairie dogs live in grasslands in North America and are known for their complex burrows. Can you help the prairie dog through the maze to the rest of its family?

START

FINISH

Read the fact files below, then try answering the
questions at the bottom of the page.

NAME: RED SQUIRREL

HABITAT:
Woodland of
Europe and
northern Asia

HOME FACT: Red
squirrels build
untidy nests in
trees using twigs
and leaves. Their
nests are lined
with soft leaves,
moss, feathers,
and hair.

NAME: HARDWICKE'S
WOOLLY BAT

HABITAT:
Forests in Borneo,
Southeast Asia

HOME FACT: This
tiny bat roosts
inside an animal-
eating pitcher
plant. The plant
feeds off the bat's
poop, while the
bat sleeps inside.

NAME: SWIFTLET

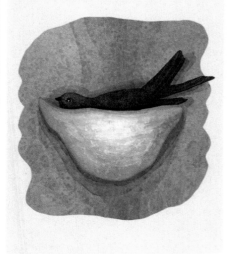

HABITAT:
Caves of Asia
and Australasia

HOME FACT:
These small
insect-eating
birds make their
homes in caves.
They create their
nests on cave
walls using their
own saliva.

NAME: SNOW LEOPARD

HABITAT:
Mountains of
central Asia

HOME FACT:
These rare
leopards shelter
among craggy
rocks and
caves on the
mountainside.
They wrap their
tails around
themselves to
keep out the cold.

1. Which animal makes its nest with its
own spit?

2. What do snow leopards use to keep
themselves warm?

3. What do swiftlets eat?

4. Which animal builds an untidy nest?

5. What type of plants do Hardwicke's woolly
bats roost in?

FINDING A MATE

When it's time to settle down and raise a family, animals do all they can to attract the healthiest mate. It's usually the male that puts on a show or fights off rivals.

Fit the missing jigsaw puzzle pieces into the correct spaces. Which two pieces are left over?

Raggiana Bird-of-Paradise

1.

2.

3.

4.

5.

6.

7.

Male birds-of-paradise are known for their beautiful feathers and for having the most elaborate displays in the animal kingdom. To impress the females, some birds display their feathers and dance, while others build structures or offer gifts.

For some creatures, finding a mate is all about fighting off the competition. Rival males challenge each other in battles where only the toughest animals win the female.

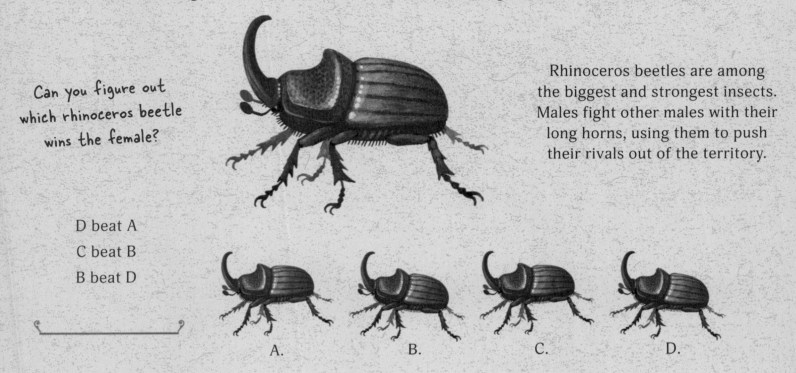

Can you figure out which rhinoceros beetle wins the female?

Rhinoceros beetles are among the biggest and strongest insects. Males fight other males with their long horns, using them to push their rivals out of the territory.

D beat A

C beat B

B beat D

A. B. C. D.

Some male invertebrates are more at risk from their mates than they are from rival males. Female praying mantises and certain types of spiders and scorpions have been known to eat their mates after the eggs have been fertilized.

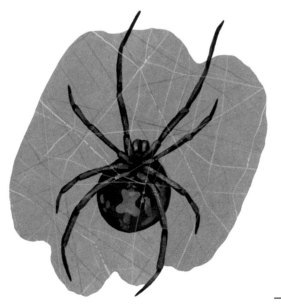

Use the code wheel to spell out a type of spider that eats her mate.

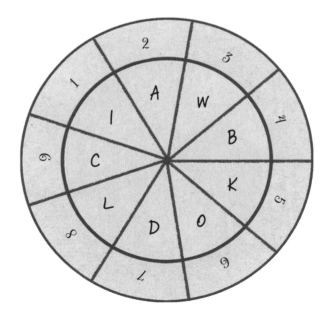

4 8 2 9 5   3 1 7 6 3

___ ___ ___ ___ ___   ___ ___ ___ ___ ___

BABY ANIMALS

The amount of time animals spend with their babies depends on the species. Some creatures lay lots of eggs, and the babies are left to hatch on their own. Other animals spend lots of time feeding and protecting their young.

Emperor penguins live in freezing Antarctica. Females lay one egg, which the father looks after. The fathers rest the egg on their feet, keeping it warm for more than two months until it hatches.

Can you find the emperor penguin that matches this one exactly?

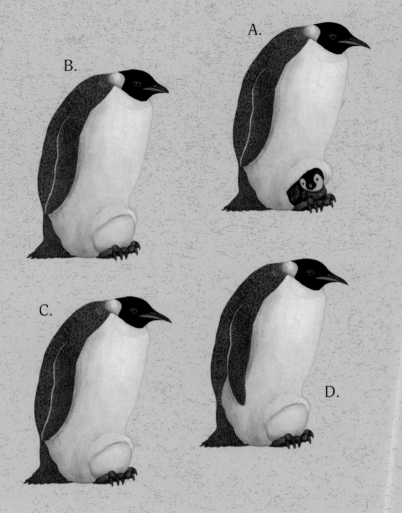

B.

A.

C.

D.

Unlike most invertebrates, scorpions do not lay eggs. Female scorpions give birth to live young called scorplings. Mothers carry their scorplings on their backs to protect them for around 20 days.

Mother scorpions can have many babies at a time. Count how many scorplings are riding on their mother's back in this picture.

Sea turtles swim ashore to lay their eggs. The mothers dig a pit for the eggs, cover them with sand to hide them, then swim away. When they hatch, the hatchlings have a long and dangerous crawl to the sea.

Can you help the hatchling turtle to the sea by following the sequence of shells below? Avoid the dangers along the way.

You can move up, down, left, and right, but not diagonally.

 1.

 2.

 3.

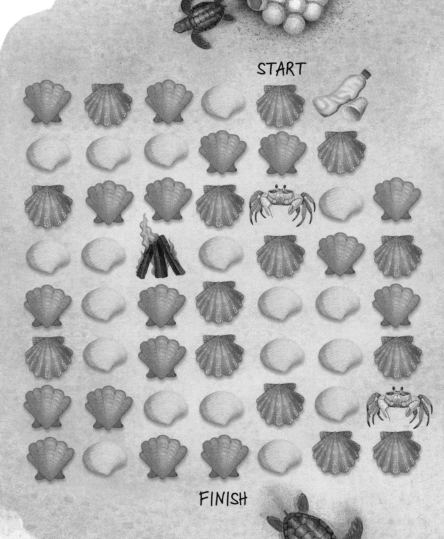

START

FINISH

Hatchlings face many dangers. Predators such as birds and crabs feed on baby turtles. Hatchlings may get tangled in trash left by humans. Lights and fires can confuse hatchlings, sending them the wrong way.

GROWING UP

Until they are grown and ready to look after themselves, young mammals are protected and cared for by their parents. Youngsters learn about the world around them by watching adults and playing with each other.

Can you complete the marsupials sudoku? Each marsupial must only appear once in each row, column, and mini square.

KANGAROO

KOALA

WOMBAT

POSSOM

Marsupials are a special kind of mammal with a pouch. The babies, called joeys, are born blind and hairless, and they stay in their mother's pouch suckling milk and growing. Most marsupials live in Australia.

Can you help this joey find its way through the maze to the safety of its mother's pouch?

When they are old enough, joeys begin to spend time out of the pouch and explore the world around them. Kangaroos are carried in their mother's pouch for about a year.

START

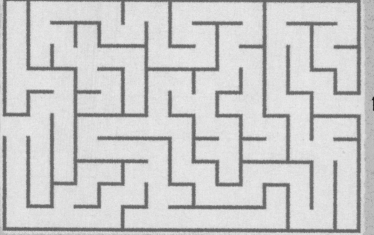

FINISH

Apart from humans, elephants spend more time looking after their young than any other animal. Elephants live in family groups, with older members of the herd helping to look after the youngsters.

Elephant calves stay with their mothers for around 10 years. Calves learn how to use their trunks by watching the older elephants.

LIVING TOGETHER

Living in a group enables animals to protect and care for each other. They may forage for food or hunt as a team. A group is also less likely to be attacked by predators, with stronger members defending the weaker ones.

Meerkats live in large groups called mobs in dry areas of southern Africa. They dig underground burrows where they rest and hide. All the adults in the mob take turns looking after the pups.

Connect the dots to complete the scene.

"Sentry" meerkats stand on their back legs keeping watch. If a predator is spotted, the sentry squeals to the rest of the mob.

A group of animals living together is given a name depending on the species.

Try this mini quiz, and see if you can work out the names given to each of these animal groups.

1. LIONS

A group of lions is called a ...

A. Pride

B. Smug

C. Legion

2. DOLPHINS

A group of dolphins is called a ...

A. Splash

B. Deluge

C. Pod

3. RHINOCEROSES

A group of rhinoceroses is called a ...

A. Thunder

B. Crash

C. Roar

4. FLAMINGOS

A group of flamingos is called a ...

A. Party

B. Parade

C. Flamboyance

Some creatures live in large colonies, with individuals doing specific jobs. They may tend to a "queen," who lays eggs, cares for young, gathers food, or protects the colony. When colonies work together in this way, they function like one large animal, or a "superorganism."

A.

B.

C.

D.

E.

F.

Can you put the picture pieces in the correct order?

Most members of a honeybee colony are worker bees. They look after the young, the queen, and the hive. Workers turn nectar from flowers into honey and use it to feed the colony.

Like bees, most ants are female workers, while the larger soldier ants fight off attackers. Drones are males who fertilize the queen's eggs. Ant colonies can contain millions of ants.

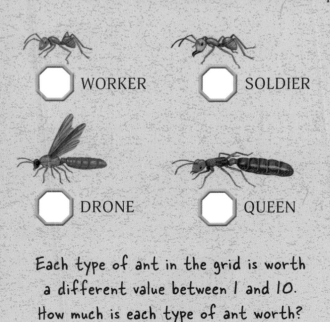

⬡ WORKER

⬡ SOLDIER

⬡ DRONE

⬡ QUEEN

Each type of ant in the grid is worth a different value between 1 and 10. How much is each type of ant worth? The total of each column has been done for you.

27 24 16 12

ANIMALS UNDER THREAT

Match each animal to its silhouette to find out the endangered status of these species.

When a type of animal is at risk of dying out, we call it endangered. Animals can become extinct for reasons such as disease, overhunting, habitat loss, and climate change. Nowadays, animals usually die out due to human activities.

MEERKAT

DODO

CRITICALLY ENDANGERED (CR) animals have an extremely high risk of becoming extinct. There are only very few left in the wild.

GIANT SQUID

KAKAPO

CRITICALLY ENDANGERED (CR)	ENDANGERED (EN)	LEAST CONCERN (LC)	EXTINCT (E)

EXTINCT ANIMALS (E) are no longer living either in the wild or as pets.

LEAST CONCERN (LC) animals are plentiful in the wild and not considered threatened.

BLACK RHINOCEROS

WILDEBEEST

AFRICAN WILD DOG

ENDANGERED ANIMALS (EN) are at high risk of becoming extinct. Their numbers are very low in the wild.

KOMODO DRAGON

FENNEC FOX

Orangutans live in forests on the Asian islands of Borneo and Sumatra. In fact, orangutan means "person of the forest" in the Malay language. These gentle apes spend most of their time in trees foraging for fruit. Sadly, orangutans are endangered due to deforestation.

Copy the picture square by square to draw your own orangutan.

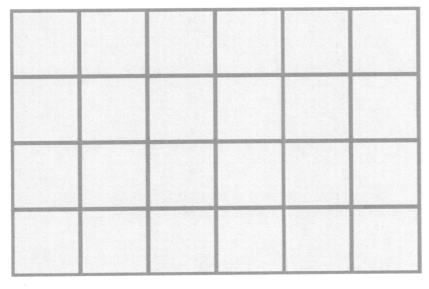

Thankfully, wildlife reserves have been created, keeping forest habitats safe for orangutans and other animals.

There are lots of things that people can do to help protect animals and their habitats.

Match the picture symbols to their descriptions to discover just a few of them.

1. _____

2. _____

3. _____

4. _____

5. _____

A. Pick up litter and recycle.

B. Raise money for wildlife charities with a bake sale.

C. Bicycle to school.

D. Save water.

E. Use less electricity.

DESERT

With so little food around, it seems unlikely that any
animal can survive the dry heat of the Sahara Desert.
Yet some creatures are cleverly adapted to live in
these scorching conditions.

Not all deserts are hot, but they are all extremely dry.
Deserts have less than 25 cm (10 in) rainfall in a year.

How many animals can you spot in the desert scene? Write the numbers in the boxes.

⬡ **ADDAX ANTELOPES** have a pale coat to reflect the sun. Their wide, flat hooves help them walk on sand.

⬡ **SCORPIONS** do not need to eat every day. They can live for up to a year without food.

⬡ **FENNEC FOXES** use their large ears to listen for prey and to get rid of excess heat in their bodies.

⬡ **FAT-TAILED GERBILS** spend the hot days in underground burrows. They hunt insects in the cool of the night.

⬡ **SANDFISH SKINK** lizards escape the heat by diving into soft sand and "swimming" with their shovel-like feet.

Draw in some extra animals to the desert scene.

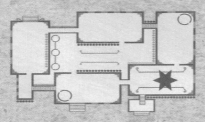

AMAZING ANIMALS

With their super senses, speed, and strength, the animal kingdom is full of record-breaking creatures. In this room, you'll discover animals with special skills and abilities. Some you have seen elsewhere in the museum, and some you haven't.

Read the fact files, then match each one to the creature it belongs to.

A. These tough water invertebrates are less than 1 mm (1/25 in) long. They can survive being baked, boiled, frozen, dried, and even sent into space.

Fastest Flier

PEREGRINE FALCON

Most Record-Breaking Animal

BLUE WHALE

Smelliest Frog

SKUNK FROG

Most Venomous Snake

INLAND TAIPAN

C. These insects make their noisy calls with a special organ called a tymbal on their abdomens. They create sounds as loud as an ambulance siren!

B. This big mammal can reach speeds of up to 114 kph (71 mph) when chasing prey. It reaches its top speed in about 3 seconds.

Best Jumper

FLEA

E. This large fish cuts through the water at speeds of 110 kph (68 mph). In its lifetime, it can swim the equivalent of eight times around the world.

D. When this speedy bird spots prey, it dives down at speeds of more than 250 kph (155 mph). That's faster than a F1 car!

Fastest Swimmer

SAILFISH

F. At 33 m (108 ft) long, these mammals are the largest animals ever. They also hold the records for largest tongue, largest heart, and loudest call.

Fastest Mammal on Land

CHEETAH

G. Every year, these birds fly from the North Pole to the South Pole and back again. They travel 71,000 km (44,000 miles) a year.

Loudest Insect

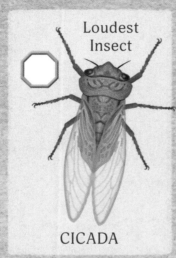

CICADA

I. Because their food contains so few nutrients, these animals snooze to conserve energy. They spend up to 22 hours a day asleep. Zzzzz ...

H. For its size, this insect is the world's strongest animal. It can pull 1,141 times its own body weight. That's like a person pulling six double-decker buses.

Longest Distance Flown

ARCTIC TERN

J. This shy but deadly reptile lives in Australia. Just one bite has enough venom to kill 100 people. Luckily, it preys on rats, rather than humans.

Greatest Animal Survivor

TARDIGRADE

Strongest Creature

DUNG BEETLE

K. This Venezuelan amphibian releases a disgusting rotten fish smell from its skin to ward off enemies. The scent is awful, but harmless.

Sleepiest Animal

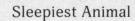

KOALA

L. These bloodsucking insects are about the size of a pinhead. Amazingly, they can jump 200 times their own body length.

THE CAMOUFLAGE EXHIBITION

The next room display contains an aquarium that looks completely empty. But is it really?

For some prey animals, hide-and-seek is a game of life-and-death. Camouflage and disguise can keep predators with even the keenest eyesight at bay. Camouflage can also be helpful to predators, allowing them to get within striking distance of prey before being discovered.

Can you find these three hidden creatures?

STONEFISH

SEA STAR

CUTTLEFISH

Camouflage is an effective protection against predators that hunt by sight—though it is less helpful against those that rely on smell or echolocation.

Some prey species have adapted over time to resemble other creatures that live in the same habitat. Looking like something poisonous is a good way to avoid being eaten!

Can you spot the nonpoisonous viceroy butterfly among the toxic monarchs?

Hint: Look closeley at the hind wings!

Some animals can change their skin tone to blend in with their environment or to stand out from the crowd. Chameleons use pigment cells to change their coloration in a flash—for communication as well as for camouflage.

Use crayons or pencils to fill in the shapes in this picture, revealing a chameleon hidden among the leaves.

ANIMAL BUILDERS

Humans aren't the only animals to build huge structures or amazing homes. Animals build nests to rear their young, snug beds to sleep in, and even soaring structures that would rival a skyscraper.

Take a look at the tailorbird's building materials. Can you figure out which picture comes next in the sequences?

Tailorbirds get their name from their ability to "sew" their nests out of leaves. They use thin strands of plants and spiderwebs for thread, and line the nests with soft things they find.

Termites are small insects that live in large colonies. They build huge mounds using spit, earth, and poop. Inside, there are tunnels, air vents, spaces for their young, food, and a royal chamber for the queen.

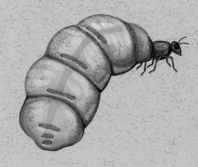

Follow the instructions to place the queen termite in her royal chamber. Draw her in the correct square.

Start at A1

Go right one square

Go up two squares

Go right two squares

Go down one square

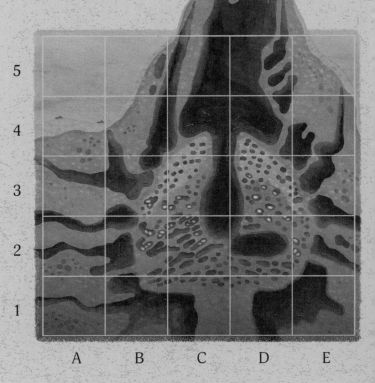

These beavers have been busy gnawing and collecting trees for their lodge. Can you figure out how many trees each beaver collected?

Beavers are one of the best-known animal builders. These large rodents live near rivers and use trees for food and building. They construct dams to form safe pools where they build their homes. Called "lodges," beaver homes have underwater entrances to keep predators out.

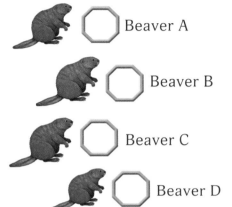

Beaver A

Beaver B

Beaver C

Beaver D

Beaver C did not collect the fewest trees.

Beaver A collected an odd number of trees.

Beaver B did not collect the most trees or the fewest trees.

Number of trees	Beaver A	Beaver B	Beaver C	Beaver D
2				
3				
4				
6				

Darwin's bark spiders produce the toughest silk of any spider, and they spin the largest webs. Their enormous webs can reach across a river and catch dozens of flying insects.

Cross out the letters W, E, and B in the web. Then rearrange the remaining letters to find out where Darwin's bark spiders live.

_ _ _ _ _ _ _ _ _ _ _

DEADLY CREATURES

Can you put the strips of the box jellyfish picture in the correct order? Strips 1 and 5 are in the correct place.

Animals can kill without the need for sharp claws and teeth. Venomous creatures inject victims with harmful chemicals that can cause pain, paralysis, or even death. Other animals are only poisonous if their toxins are eaten by another creature.

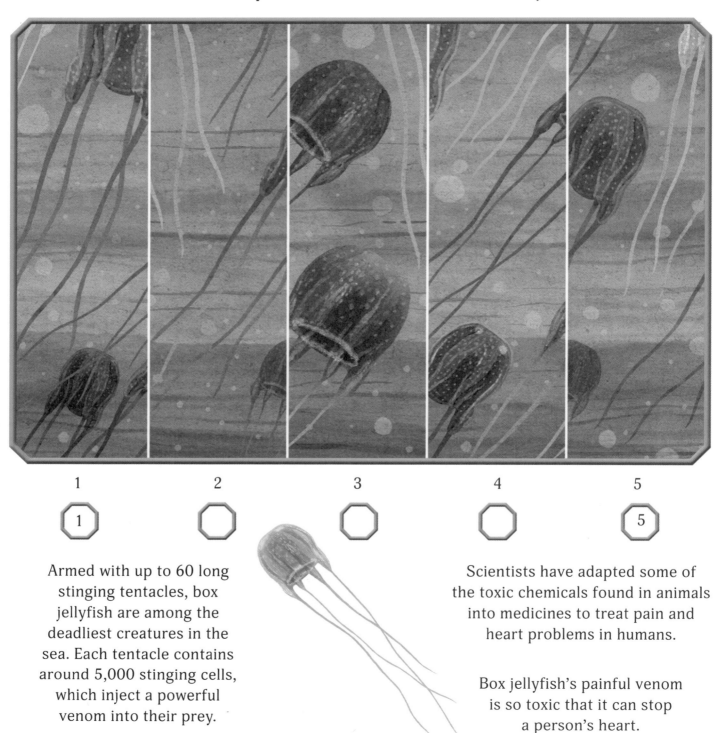

1   2   3   4   5

1   ○   ○   ○   5

Armed with up to 60 long stinging tentacles, box jellyfish are among the deadliest creatures in the sea. Each tentacle contains around 5,000 stinging cells, which inject a powerful venom into their prey.

Scientists have adapted some of the toxic chemicals found in animals into medicines to treat pain and heart problems in humans.

Box jellyfish's painful venom is so toxic that it can stop a person's heart.

Poison dart frogs are some of the most toxic animals on Earth. Most poison dart frogs have vivid markings to warn potential predators not to eat them. Rather than making their own poison, the toxins in the frogs' skin come from the insects they eat.

PHANTASMAL POISON FROG

Design your own poisonous frog—make sure you use your brightest pens!

DYEING POISON FROG

GOLDEN POISON FROG

The most poisonous of all is the golden poison frog. This amphibian is smaller than your pinky finger but contains enough toxins to kill 10 people.

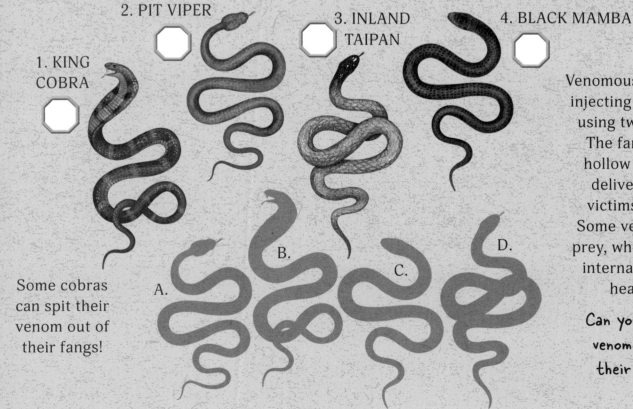

2. PIT VIPER

3. INLAND TAIPAN

4. BLACK MAMBA

1. KING COBRA

Venomous snakes hunt by injecting toxic chemicals using two sharp fangs. The fangs are either hollow or grooved to deliver venom into victims as they bite. Some venoms paralyze prey, while others cause internal bleeding and heart attacks.

Some cobras can spit their venom out of their fangs!

A.

B.

C.

D.

Can you match these venomous snakes to their silhouettes?

MIGRATION

Each year, some animals group together to go on a long and often perilous journey called a migration. Animals migrate in order to escape from the cold, find food, breed and raise young, or all three.

Read all about these different migrating animals. Then put them in order of distance covered, with 1 being the longest.

1 ....
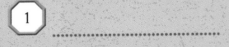

2 ....

3 ....
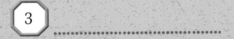

4 ....
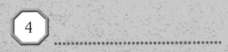

Scientists believe that some migrating animals find their way by following the Sun, Moon, or stars, or by sensing the Earth's magnetic field.

MONARCH BUTTERFLIES

Millions of monarch butterflies fly up to 4,800 km (3,000 miles) from Canada to Mexico every year to escape from the cold. They spend the winter resting on fir trees. In the spring, the monarchs lay their eggs.

WILDEBEEST

Huge herds of around 500,000 wildebeests travel 1,600 km (1,000 miles) across the African plains to find fresh grass to eat. The herd can stretch 40 km (25 miles) long.

ARCTIC TERNS

It is always summer for Arctic terns! These birds migrate between the Arctic circle and Antarctica to escape from the harshest weather. They travel at least 30,000 km (18,600 miles) each way.

LEATHERBACK TURTLES

Bigger than a human, leatherbacks are the largest type of sea turtle. All sea turtles migrate to lay their eggs. Leatherbacks travel the farthest, at around 6,000 km (3,700 miles) each way.

The migration of many millions of Christmas Island crabs is a spectacular sight. Although they live in forests, the bright-red crabs only breed in the sea. The crabs must cross roads and avoid being eaten by predators on their journey.

Can you spot seven differences between the two pictures?

THE BIG SNOOZE

To get through winter, some animals migrate to warmer places, some grow thicker fur and hoard food, and others hibernate. Hibernating animals find or make a resting place, then go into a sleeplike state for the coldest weeks or months of the year.

All the animals listed below either hibernate or become inactive for shorter periods to save energy. Can you find each animal in the word search?

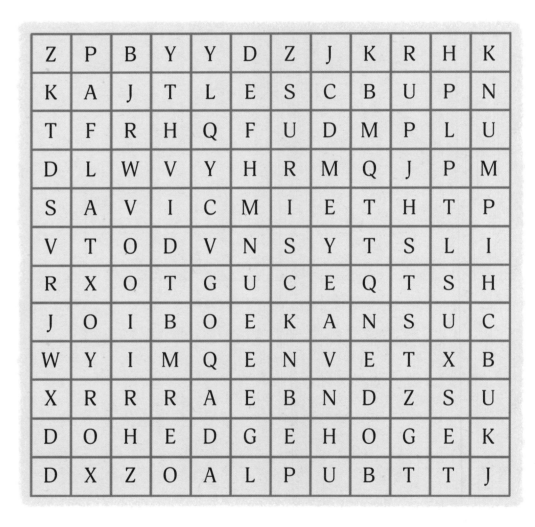

Z	P	B	Y	Y	D	Z	J	K	R	H	K
K	A	J	T	L	E	S	C	B	U	P	N
T	F	R	H	Q	F	U	D	M	P	L	U
D	L	W	V	Y	H	R	M	Q	J	P	M
S	A	V	I	C	M	I	E	T	H	T	P
V	T	O	D	V	N	S	Y	T	S	L	I
R	X	O	T	G	U	C	E	Q	T	S	H
J	O	I	B	O	E	K	A	N	S	U	C
W	Y	I	M	Q	E	N	V	E	T	X	B
X	R	R	R	A	E	B	N	D	Z	S	U
D	O	H	E	D	G	E	H	O	G	E	K
D	X	Z	O	A	L	P	U	B	T	T	J

BAT

BEAR

BUTTERFLY

CHIPMUNK

DORMOUSE

HEDGEHOG

HUMMINGBIRD

SNAKE

TOAD

WOODCHUCK

Hummingbirds go into a kind of mini hibernation called torpor every day.

When animals hibernate, they're not sleeping. Their body temperature drops, and breathing and heart rate slows down. By slowing down their bodies, animals save energy.

Which picture matches the hibernating dormouse exactly?

Hazel dormice are small rodents that live in European hedgerows and woodlands. To survive winter, the dormice load up on nuts and berries. Then they make a round nest of leaves and grass and hibernate for around six months.

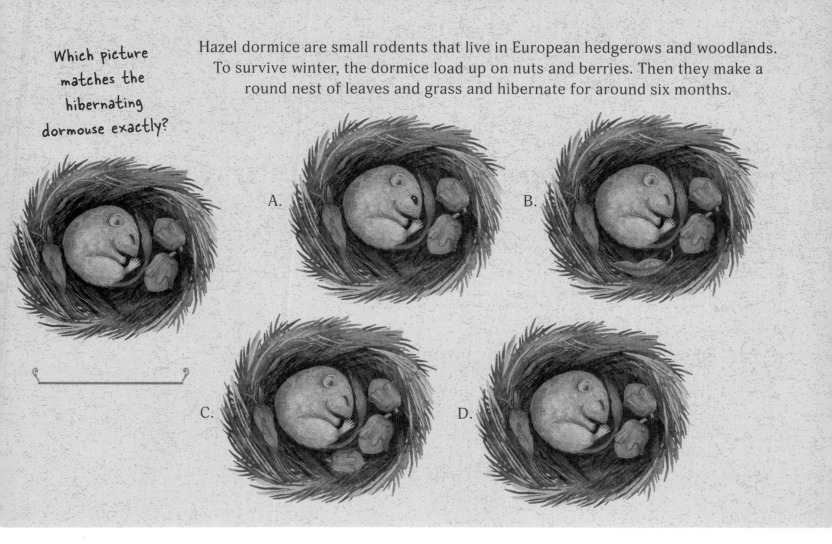

A.

B.

C.

D.

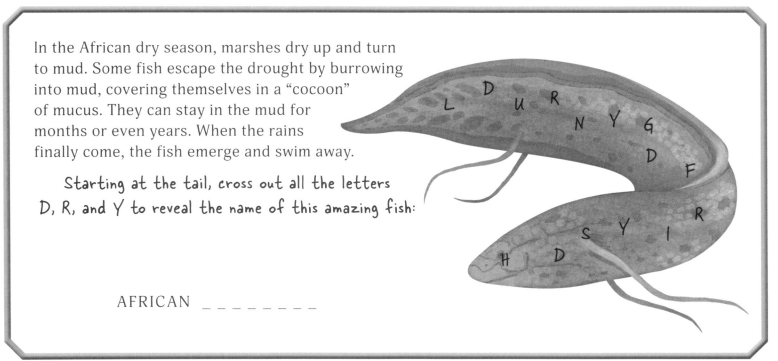

In the African dry season, marshes dry up and turn to mud. Some fish escape the drought by burrowing into mud, covering themselves in a "cocoon" of mucus. They can stay in the mud for months or even years. When the rains finally come, the fish emerge and swim away.

Starting at the tail, cross out all the letters D, R, and Y to reveal the name of this amazing fish:

AFRICAN _ _ _ _ _ _ _

SPECIAL SKILLS

From the depths of the oceans to the skies above us, the world is full of incredible creatures doing remarkable things. This collection of animals has some very unusual abilities and clever tricks.

Axolotls are strange-looking amphibians with amazing abilities. If they are injured, axolotls can grow back parts of their bodies, including tails, limbs, and even parts of their heart and brain!

Can you match the axolotls into exact pairs?

A.
B.
C.
D.
E.
F.
G.
H.

This shrimp hunts by snapping its claw, shooting out a powerful air bubble. As it pops, the air in the bubble is nearly as hot as the Sun's surface and makes a sound louder than a gunshot! The shrimp uses its weapon to stun prey.

Count 3 letters back in the alphabet from each letter below to reveal the type of shrimp.

S L V W R O

Bioluminescent animals are creatures that can make their own light in their bodies. They do this for reasons such as defending against predators, attracting mates, and luring prey. Many deep-sea animals are bioluminescent.

Can you match each bioluminescent sea creature to its description?

○ 1. COMB JELLY

○ 2. ANGLERFISH

○ 3. LANTERNFISH

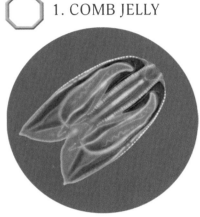

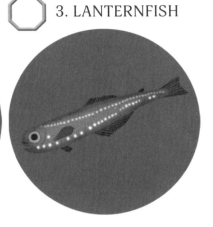

A. This scary-looking fish has a dangling spine on its head that lights up to attract prey.

B. This deep-sea fish uses light organs on its head, body, and tail to signal to mates.

C. This creature has a see-through body that glows to distract potential predators.

Fireflies, or lightning bugs, are bioluminescent beetles. They make their light by mixing chemicals in their abdomens. They glow to attract a mate and to warn predators.

Complete the jigsaw puzzle. Can you figure out which piece doesn't fit?

1.

2.

3.

4.

HABITAT EXHIBITION:

URBAN

Under the cover
of darkness, some
creatures take to the
streets to look for food.

Nocturnal animals are only active
at night. Creatures that come
out at dusk and dawn are called
crepuscular, while daytime
animals are known as diurnal.

How many of these night-loving creatures can you find in the scene? Can you spot two more creatures hiding?

SLUGS need to keep their bodies moist, so they come out at night. They are hunted by birds, frogs, and small mammals.

MOTHS feed on nectar and are important plant pollinators. They are drawn to lights in the dark.

HEDGEHOGS eat slugs, beetles, and other invertebrates.

Urban **FOXES** prefer to eat meat but will eat almost anything, including food that people throw away.

BATS are the only mammals capable of true flight. They feed on insects.

PUZZLE ANSWERS

PAGE 6:
1. D; 2. F; 3. C; 4. E; 5. A; 6. B

PAGE 7:

Invertebrates: 6,
Fish: 4,
Amphibians: 2,
Reptiles: 4,
Birds: 5,
Mammals: 4

PAGE 8:

PAGE 9:

MOTH   HOVERFLY   BUMBLEBEE   BEETLE

PAGE 10:
1. C; 2. D; 3. A; 4. B
Jigsaw piece 5 doesn't fit.

PAGE 11:

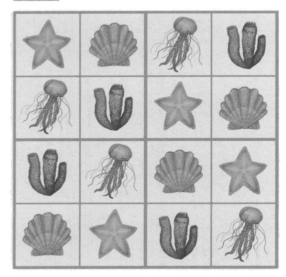

Silhouette B matches the main picture of the squid.

PAGE 12:
RED SNAPPER
There are 21 Atlantic herring in the school.

PAGE 13:
1. Whale shark; 2. Oarfish; 3. Great white shark;
4. Ocean sunfish; 5. Humphead wrasse

PAGE 14:

D is the toad hiding among the frogs.

PAGE 15:
Frogspawn: E2, G1, and H3
Tadpoles: B2, C2, and D2
Water lily: A6 and D5

The mudskipper is not an amphibian—it is a fish!

PAGE 16:
D.

PAGE 17:

PAGE 18:

There are 13 flamingos.

1. E; 2. F; 3. C; 4. D; 5. A; 6. G; 7. B

PAGE 19:
SWIFT

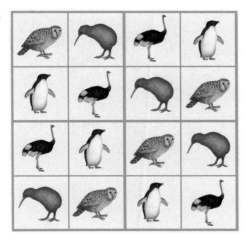

PAGE 20:
A.5; B.3; C.1; D.2; E.6; F.4

PAGE 21:
The Cuvier's beaked whale can hold its breath for 222 minutes.

Flying fox is a type of bat.

PAGES 22–23:

- Bullet ants: 4
- Red-eyed tree frogs: 5
- Spider monkeys: 5
- **Macaws: 6**
- Tree runner lizards: 3

Other animals:
- Butterflies: 4
- Bee hummingbird: 1
- Anaconda: 1
- Jaguar: 1
- Three-toed sloth: 1

PAGE 24:
1.H, 2H, 3.C, 4.H, 5.C, 6.O, 7.O, 8.O, 9.C

PAGE 25:

Z	N	O	M	L	A	S	B
T	A	G	B	I	T	B	E
Q	I	R	A	C	Z	S	R
Z	Q	U	E	E	T	Y	R
T	D	S	R	O	K	G	I
O	N	U	O	F	F	S	E
I	G	R	A	S	S	E	S
E	S	O	O	M	R	V	M

Vulture
Dung beetle

PAGE 26:

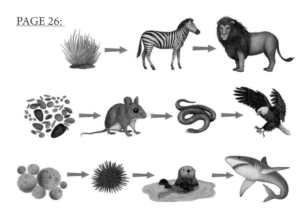

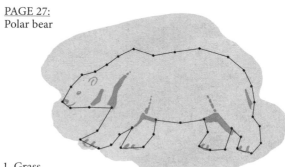

PAGE 27:
Polar bear

1. Grass
2. Kestrel and fox
3. Grasshopper and caterpillar

PAGE 28:
Roadrunners can run 12 steps in one second.

Picture C matches the praying mantis.

PAGE 29:
E3

A, B, and C are all true!

PAGE 30:
17

1. D; 2. C; 3. A; 4. B

PAGE 31:

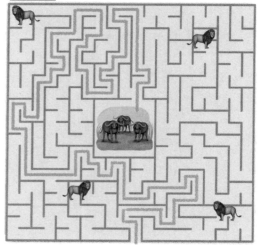

PAGE 32:

Hours: 4

Hours: 3

Hours: 5
Total hours = 12

There are 14 goats in the picture. If each has 2 kids, there are 28 kids (14 x 2 = 28). Add the original 14, and there are 42 goats in the herd (14 + 28 = 42).

PAGE 33:

An animal that eats mostly fruit is a C. Frugivore.

PAGE 34:

2, 5, 1, 4, 3

	Zebra	Wildebeest	Hare
Clan 1	X	✓	X
Clan 2	✓	X	X
Clan 3	X	X	✓

A. Dingo, B. African wild dog, C. Grey, or gray wolf

PAGE 36:
1. False. Armadillos eat mostly insects, such as termites.
2. True.
3. False. Armadillos live in warm places, such as rain forests, grasslands, and semideserts.
4. True.

A. tortoise
B. turtle

PAGE 37:

A	B	C	D	E	F	G	H	I	J	K	L	M	N	O	P	Q	R	S	T	U	V	W	X	Y	Z
3	4	5	6	7	8	9	10	11	12	13	14	15	16	17	18	19	20	21	22	23	24	25	26	27	28

21	5	3	14	18	7	14
S	C	A	L	P	E	L

SCALPEL

PAGES 38–39:

- ○ 3 Walruses
- ○ 11 Harp seals
- ○ 2 Polar bears
- ○ 2 Orcas
- ○ 9 Arctic cod

PAGE 40:
1. D, 2. C, 3. E, 4. A, 5. B

PAGE 41:

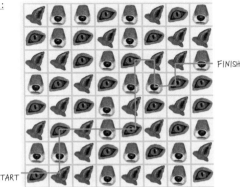

C.

PAGE 42:
200

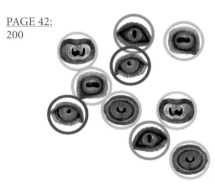

1. A and I, 2. F and C, 3. D and E, 4. B and H, 5. G and J

PAGE 43:
A and B are exactly the same size.

PAGE 44:
NOSE-LEAF

1. A; 3. C; 4. B
Jigsaw piece 2 doesn't fit.

PAGE 45:
1. long-eared jerboa, 2. wolf, 3. African elephant, 4. hare, 5. caracal.

PAGE 46:

MOSQUITO   KOALA   SHARK

SILK MOTH   VULTURE   EEL

PAGE 47:

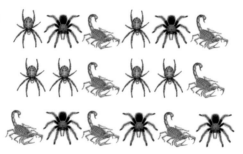

B

PAGE 48:
Cow: 25,000; Chicken: 30; Rabbit: 17,000; Lion: 450; Pig: 15,000

PAGE 49:
17
C

PAGE 50:

PAGE 51:

  A.3—walrus

  B.4—star-nosed mole

  C.1—rat

  D.2–common, or harbour/harbor seal

PAGE 52:
Square E3

PAGE 53:

PAGES 54–55:

○ Manta ray: 1
◉ Clownfish: 3
○ Finger corals: 5
◉ Banded sea kraits: 2
○ Butterfly fish: 11

○ Sea stars: 3

PAGE 56:
1C;
2F;
3E;
4B;
5D;
6A

PAGE 57:
ZEBRA—FOAL = 1. H
TURTLE—HATCHLING = 8. C
SWAN—CYGNET = 2. F
FROG—TADPOLE = 6. B
BUTTERFLY—CATERPILLAR = 3. A
RHINOCEROS—CALF = 4. G
SEAL—PUP = 7. D
KANGAROO—JOEY = 5. E

Adwaita lived to be 256 years old.

PAGE 58:
1. E; 2. B; 3. C;
4. D; 5. A

PAGE 59:
1. Swiftlet
2. Their tails
3. Insects
4. Red squirrel
5. Pitcher plants

PAGE 60:
A 5; B 3; C 2; D 1; E 7

Jigsaw puzzle pieces 4 and 6 are left over.

PAGE 61:
Rhinoceros beetle C wins the female.

BLACK WIDOW

PAGE 62:
C.

There are 12 scorplings.

PAGE 63:

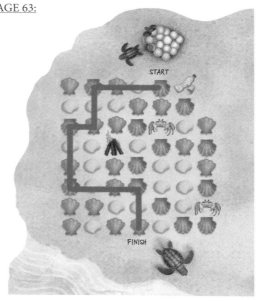

PAGE 64:

PAGE 65:

PAGE 66:

1. A
2. C
3. B
4. C

PAGE 67:

D.   F.   B.

A.   E.   C.

Worker: 3; Soldier: 5; Drone: 7; Queen: 10

PAGE 68:
Critically endangered:
Black rhinoceros; Kakapo; Meerkat; Fennec fox

Endangered:
African wild dog; Komodo dragon

Least concern:
Giant squid; Wildebeest

Extinct:
Dodo

PAGE 69:

 A.   B.

 C.   D.   E.

PAGES 70–71:

- 7 Addax antelopes
- 4 Scorpions
- 3 Fennec foxes
- 4 Fat-tailed gerbils
- 2 Sandfish skinks

Page 72–73:
A—Tardigrade
B —Cheetah
C—Cicada
D—Peregrine falcon
E—Sailfish
F—Blue whale
G—Arctic tern
H—Dung beetle
I—Koala
J—Inland taipan
K—Skunk frog
L—Flea

PAGE 74:

PAGE 75:

PAGE 76:

D2

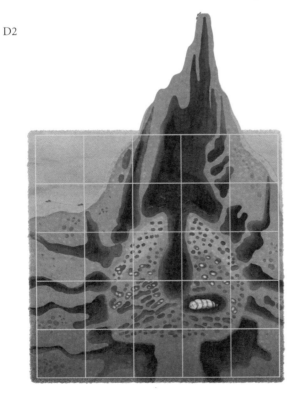

PAGE 77:

Number of trees	Beaver A	Beaver B	Beaver C	Beaver D
2	x	x	x	✓
3	✓	x	x	x
4	x	✓	x	x
6	x	x	✓	x

Beaver A: 3
Beaver B: 4
Beaver C: 6
Beaver D: 2

Darwin's bark spiders live in MADAGASCAR.

PAGE 78:

1, 4, 3, 2, 5

PAGE 79:
1. B; 2. A; 3. D; 4. C

PAGE 80:
1. Arctic terns
2. Leatherback turtles
3. Monarch butterflies
4. Wildebeest

PAGE 81:

PAGE 82:

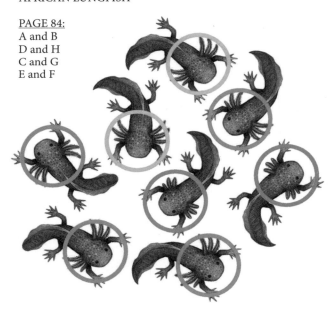

Z	P	B	Y	Y	D	Z	J	K	R	H	K
K	A	J	T	L	E	S	C	B	U	P	N
T	F	R	H	Q	F	U	D	M	P	L	U
D	L	W	V	Y	H	R	M	Q	J	P	M
S	A	V	I	C	M	I	E	T	H	T	P
V	T	O	D	V	N	S	Y	T	S	L	I
R	X	O	T	G	U	C	E	Q	T	S	H
J	O	I	B	O	E	K	A	N	S	U	C
W	Y	I	M	Q	E	N	V	E	T	X	B
X	R	R	R	A	E	B	N	D	Z	S	U
D	O	H	E	D	G	E	H	O	G	E	K
D	X	Z	O	A	L	P	U	B	T	T	J

PAGE 83:
D

AFRICAN LUNGFISH

PAGE 84:
A and B
D and H
C and G
E and F

PISTOL

PAGE 85:
1. C
2. A
3. B

4. A; 2. B; 1. C
Jigsaw puzzle piece 3 doesn't fit.

PAGES 86–87:

○ Foxes: 2
○ Hedgehog: 1
○ Bats: 3
○ Slugs: 2
○ Moths: 5

Other animals:
○ Rat: 1
○ Beetle: 1
○ Owl: 1